PEARLS
OF
WISDOM

LINDA MAE FOSTER

Xulon
PRESS

Pearls Of Wisdom
by Linda Mae Foster

Printed in the United States of America.

ISBN 9781498456012

www.xulonpress.com

TABLE OF CONTENTS

ACKNOWLEDGEMENTS

I would like to thank my daughter Loreal McAbee for her support all of these years who stayed with me in this long journey. I also would like to thank my parents Leona and Roy Foster, and my grandmother Laurita Bivins who made their transition to glory. They instilled Christian values in me at a very young age which has inspired me to write these poems and be a blessing and encouragement to others.

LINDA M. FOSTER

A PRAYER OF COMPLETENESS

Lord, grant me a sense of direction
That I may discern good from evil

Lord, grant me wisdom
That I may increase in knowledge
And understanding

Lord, grant me honesty and sincerity
That I may maintain the knowledge
Of truth and false

Lord, grant me purity
And an oneness with You
And never ever
Let it come apart
That I may gain
A sacred heart

AUTHOR: Linda M. Foster
Dated: 4/8/2000

A SHADOW OF THE PAST

As I sit upon my bed
My eyes glance through a crowded room
The pain in my heart makes me feel
That I am doomed

I am afraid to face this lonely day
With the fears of the loss of tomorrow
Although my tears are few it is not my
Place to give for those tears I had to borrow

My memories shall linger on
And my thoughts shall not diminish
My love shall sustain
And my joy shall remain

Even though my hands ache to touch
My eyes desire to look upon
And my heart rushes to be near
I sure hope that I can be of good cheer

Although my hopes and dreams were shattered
And my expectations were scattered
My body was not battered

Be still my heart
Although we must be apart
There's a special place for me in his heart

I don't know if he will ever forget
I can't predict
But I will admit he will always remember
A shadow of the past

Author: Linda M. Foster
Dated: 3/20/1999

A TIME SPENT ALONE

It's time to go alone
Even though sometimes
This rocky road that I must cross
Seems hard to mend

Just like a shattered picture to a frame
A missing piece to a puzzle
My life has now become
Many who I have trusted
Had deceived me
In pretending they were my friends
The ones who I tried constantly
Every day not to offend

But for now I must cry alone
As though I wept not
Nevertheless my future stands secure
My footsteps towards the mark
Are very sure
My hurtful past I must now leave behind
Forgiving those
And removing
Treacherous thoughts in remembering when
As the grace and mercies of God compassed about me
While I put my trust in Thee

Harmless to say
Now I have chosen a new and greater way
Leaving my own principles
Trying to please others
And gain the respect
From the One
Who rules above
By giving Himself

continued

He has shown love

Now that seed
Remains in the Earth
It has been sown

Now I too must walk
Along this road
Even as He did
That day alone

Author: Linda M. Foster
Dated: 6/6/1999

A WORD OF TIME IN SEASON

God told me who I was
Therefore I am somebody more than a conquer through Him
that loved me
He has given me a glow that cover girl can't touch
A blemish blush cannot cover up
He has given me an understanding
Along with that knowledge
Then came wisdom
That's something money cannot buy
Silver, rubies and all the fine gold
Nothing can be compared unto it

After your day has ended and you are from the driver's seat
of your car
As you enter your home and the shades are being pulled down
You proceed to your bedroom
Kick the shoes off thy feet
Strip yourself from your garments
When you have laid your head upon your pillow

In the early wee hours of the morning
While each string of hair is out of place
You stroll to the bathroom
Your eyes glance for the mirror
Who are you?
When no one else is watching, who are you then?
Your clothes do not tell you who you are
Your heart does

Some people think they are impressing God by what they wear
What they drive
How much money they have
Where they live
When someone else is less fortunate, they seem to belittle them
They become boastful

continued

And proud

Words from the wise
Verily I say unto you
Who are you trying to impress?
You don't impress Me
You don't clothe Me
I clothe you
What can you give unto Me?
Nothing but your heart
You came into this world with nothing so that's
the way you will leave
From dust you came and from the dust ye shall return

Written by: Linda Foster
Date: 2/20/2013

ABANDONED TEARS

Tears are sometimes a sign of releasing
And a time of rejoicing

Tears are not a sign of weakness as some suppose
It can be a cleansing
To whom it is given knows

Tears are given to everyone
It can be used with past mistakes
And heartaches

Tears are normally seen when there is pain and sorrow
But yet there is still hope for tomorrow
Tears can be joy and laughter
You'll find that it can be healthier after

Tears can be a symbol of restoration
one towards another
Or appreciation one towards another

Tears are mostly misunderstood by mankind
That's why a lot of men lose their mind

Tears bring many to fear
And some of good cheer
But they all are so dear
Because they are abandoned tears

AUTHOR: Linda M. Foster
Dated: 1/14/2000

CALL UPON ME

Call upon Me
I'll answer you
Talk to Me
I will hear you

Praise Thee
You'll be lifted up
Thou bones shall be made fat
Years enhanced to many
Life indulges plenty

Fast from meats
I'll break the bands
Fast from television
I will control your life
Fast your time
I'll be in you a well of water
Springing up to everlasting life

Abstain from evil
Rejoice in good
Hope is for tomorrow
Life contains today

Sustain thyself
Sell out
Keep thou praise as pure as the snow
That cometh down from Heaven then tilts and covers the ground
Until that day appointed

AUTHOUR: Linda M. Foster
DATE: 5/10/1998

CARE FREE

God will take care of it all
No matter what others may say or do
I know He will see me through
God will take care of it all

When trouble comes my way
He will truly stay
Where can I run?
Right into Your arms
God will take care of me and you

Destruction in the land
Please hold my hand
God will take care of it all

Amen

AUTHOR: Linda M. Foster
Date: April 27, 2013

CLEAN HANDS

Blow the trumpet
Cry aloud
And spare not
Show my people their ways

Though their sin are like scarlet
They shall be white as snow
Though they are red like crimson
They shall be as wool

Blow the trumpet
In Zion
Sound the alarm
On My Holy mountain
Tell God's people everywhere
Tell them to clean their hands

AUTHOR: Linda M. Foster
Dated: 4/7/2000

COME DINE WITH ME

I am captivated by your smile
Your beauty
Your warmth
Your charm
Your tenderness
Your meekness
Your gentleness
And your humility
I am blown away by your kiss
Fascinated by your touch of style
You have Me
Come in and dine with Me at My table for
I have been waiting for you
You are the rose pedals around My table for I am the vine
Your are the branches
Come break bread with Me and drink from My cup
For I am the Bread of Life which came down from Heaven
Put your hand in the palm of Mine
where your face is forever embezzled in My memory
Come lie with Me on the green grass near the
clear streams of still waters
Lay your head upon My breast and rest for I careth for you
Be rooted and grounded
Forever abide continually in My love
Be like the tree planted by the rivers of water that
bring forth fruit in it's season
Your leaf shall not whither and whatever you do shall prosper
I will go before you and make the crooked places straight and
the rough places smooth
I will walk ahead of you and watch you from behind
As My eyes gaze upon you, I see that you are precious
in My sight
Verily I say unto you again come break bread with Me
Let Me take you to a place where you have never been before
For you are My precious precious bride

AUTHOR: Linda M. Foster
Date: 2/20/13

COME LET US REASON TOGETHER

O, come let us grow old together
Come grow old together with me
Let our gray hair satisfy thee with old age
And that our speech be seasoned with sweet whis-
pers of wisdom
While the corns on each foot grow longer and longer
As each step we take
Gets shorter and shorter with distance

O, come let us break bread together
Come break bread with me
May it be seasoned with purpose
Always smooth continually
On every side
See that the wine is always imported
To insure the mixture of all kinds of
Different fruits

O, come let us make music together
Songs of songs
While the angels sing
And the robin flapped their wings
Come and ye shall see
O, come make heavenly music together with me

Author: Linda M. Foster
Dated: 10/15/2000

DADDY'S LITTLE GIRL

I remember daddy
I remember you
You were oh so true
I remember you
My heart cries for you
I remember you
Just because I can't spend my time with you
I remember you

I wish I can call you on the phone
And tell you the good news
How my life turned to new
I know I shouldn't cry the tears of sorrow
For being without you tomorrow
I know I should hold back my fears of past years
I had to borrow selfishly

I hold you close to my heart
As if you were gone yesterday
Many years have gone by
Foolishly some would dare to say
I cry because I can't say goodbye
Needless to say I remember your shame and the pain
You had to bear on Earth

I know that one day I'll be able to see you again
Although this is all true
There's one more thing I'd like to add
Even though your sorrows and sadness has disappeared
I cry because I cannot spend time with you

Words from the wise
One day I'll hear these words
Why do ye search for the living among the dead

continued

He is not here
He has risen
Just as Christ said He would
Now therefore I will comfort myself
In remembering these words

AUTHOR: Linda M. Foster
Dated: 12/21/13

EMOTIONALLY HANDICAPPED

Handicapped in the natural means leaning on
someone or something for support
Some lean on wheelchairs or canes
It helps them to keep moving forward
Therefore they'll keep making progress
On the other hand emotionally handicapped is leaning
on the support of other people
Standing in a crowd with people who surrounds you and gives
you a sense of worth and value
Then again there are some who lean on
how they look on the outside to determine their value and worth

Some lean on material things
What they own in life makes them feel popular
People who tend to lean on materials to make them
feel important
Often times become judgmental and critical
Not leaving out hypocrisy
They appear pleasant on the outside but on the inside
they're rotten to the core

All the above leads to pride
Pride is one of the seven things that God hates
When they reach this peak they have entered into the danger zone
They shall surely fall
The bible says pride goes before destruction
and a haughty spirit before a fall

I'm glad I have come to realize that some people
With this problem feel they have not yet reached their expectation
Maybe even longing for someone else's approval
Trying to fill a void of insecurities
Many may feel like they are less important

continued

Waiting on someone to recognize that they are

If no one does they sometimes lash out at others
Who are less fortunate than they are
When you know who you are
There's no need for someone to validate you
You don't have to make someone feel bad
In order to make yourself feel better

Author: Linda M. Foster
Dated: 11/6/1999

FALSELY ACCUSED

While lying horizontally across my bed
My mind wonders
Thoughts of yesterday fills my heart and bleeds my soul

On the night in question I was accused falsely
A vicious rumor had spread against me
There is a saying I was wounded in the house
of my family and familiar friends

The rumor that was spread against me
could cause me to have a bad name
or even destroy my character
The Good Book says a good name is rather to be chosen
than great riches

I stand firmly today on what I know to be true
I choose not to entangle myself
Or even prove the lie of the rumor
I am not going to fight for my innocence
Or even retaliate against the one who
deliberately accused me falsely

Although there are some people who will believe
this untruth because they
would rather believe a lie than the truth
simply because it's gossip

Some people would rather believe the worst than the best
Because their own deeds were evil
But then again there are some people who are strong minded
They let it go in one ear and out the other

continued

We as people should judge our neighbors on what
we know and love about them
And not build trust on a rumor from someone who
accuses falsely
For misery loves company
You should judge a person on how he or she treats you
Not on how people claim they treat them

Now to say this rumor does not bother me
is to say that I am without feelings
Nevertheless it may affect what's around me
But it wont destroy what's inside me
I am who I am and that's who I'll stay
No matter what comes my way

Now unto thee accuser
You deliberately lied against me
I could retaliate or even do the same thing
that was done unto me
But I know truth prevails

A lie can only travel so far
Then it comes to a stop
For example
You can plant a seed
If you don't water or feed it
It can't grow
It dies
So shall a lie

I choose not to mingle in your world
You live in yours
And I shall live in mine

AUTHOR: Linda M. Foster
Date: 4/8/1999

FATHER'S LOVE

A father's love secures you
It's designed purpose is to
train you up in the way that you should go
For when you are old
He or she will not depart from the truth

A father's love is stability
Every child needs a father
For many had walked away
And left their children behind
It's as if they lost their mind

A father's love is all the above and more
So you say that your dad has evened the score?
Well I can tell that you are fine
For you have a father
Just like mine

AUTHOR: Linda M. Foster
Dated: 8/5/2000

FEAR NOT

Be not afraid
He has given His Angels charge concerning thee
Less thou be discomforted

Fret not thyself because of evil doers
Never be discontent
For the Lord upholds the right in heart

Surely He brings them to safety
Therefore they are kept from fear and harm
Fear not for the Lord thy God is with thee
Even unto the end

Author: Linda M. Foster
Dated: 12/20/2013

FEELINGS ARE MUTUAL

Feelings are an emotion
It's something you can feel
Feelings can be crushed
But in time they will heal

Feelings is sometimes an argument
That is given by choice
Just as a decision is made
To choose a Rolls Royce

Feelings are also shared by two
For the love of many it is still new
I write this poem for the two of you
Because you are the one out of a few

Feelings between the two of you
Are as one
Your thoughts, your dreams,
And your expectations

Feelings between the both of you
Some say it's crucial
But I say unto you
It's feelings that are mutual

AUTHOR: Linda M. Foster
Dated: 6/3/2000

FORGIVENESS IS DIVINE

Forgiveness is like the peace and quiet
that comes from up above
It's pure
And it rest upon you like a dove

Forgiveness allows you to sit in Heavenly places
Where you can behold the Angels faces

Forgiveness is less mentioned
But needs to pay close attention

Forgiveness eases the pain of a wounded heart
Come on, be smart
You can have a brand new start

Forgiveness causes you to have sweet sleep
And your joy you shall keep
Some prefer to repay
Other's say
It's my dime
And it's a waste of time
But yet true forgiveness is divine

AUTHOR: Linda M. Foster
DATED: 5/2/2000

FRIENDS ARE FOREVER

Friends are forever
He who walks away
Now stands alone

You say I have others
If you can't conquer those who are near
How can you run with those
Make font size same as rest of text

Author: Linda M. Foster
Date: 3/10/2001

GIVE UNTO CAESAR

Give unto Caesar the thing's that are Caesar's
And give God the things that are His
This is the statement that Jesus used when
being tempted of the Pharisees
This is a true saying
Many people forget that God uses people to help them
along life's way
They give praise to God and none to the one He used to help them
Therefore they become offended by feeling not appreciated
and used up
Although we all know that God is the source of all good things
that happen unto us
But even in all that it's okay to say thank you
I appreciate your help

Now the conclusion of the whole matter is this
If we don't start showing appreciation towards people who has
helped us along the way
When we need their help again some may turn a deaf ear to our cry
Their hearts will turn cold
So you see it's better to give credit unto whom credit is due
Than to say I thank God only
It don't take any gratitude from the Father
Or make your appreciation of Him any less
It is God's will that we give thanks
in all things

AUTHOR: Linda M. Foster
Date: 11/5/2013

GOD SHOW YOUR LOVE

A time of pain wandering through the wilderness
makes me wonder why the day is dark and gloomy
Smiles hidden from the sunny skies and bright moon
Longing for some answers to questions why
As the dust clings to the bottom of my feet
My mouth is dry and parched while drifting deeper
into life's problems

Although I didn't thirst for water I surely wish that rain will fall
Living today pressing toward the agony of tomorrow
faded dreams of passing the time away
Oh how I wish some rain will fall
How I pray that love will cover me and hide me from the
trouble that surrounds me
May it shield and protect me with the armor of truth
Let it abide with me forever more 'till all loneliness in me subside

AUTHOR: Linda M. foster
Dated: 12/20/13

HE CALLED ME FRIEND

I was born in a world of sin
I had no hope within
You came along and rescued me
And then You called me friend

In this dying world of sorrow
You found me on that day at Calvary
You stood in my place

How could this be?
A King died for me
Oh what manner of love He has bestowed upon me
I find it hard to believe
A King would die for me
Then arose and called me friend

AUTHOR: Linda M. Foster
Dated: 12/21/2000

HEART OF DEEP WATER

As I lay across my bed
Tears of discomfort
Fills my heart
And floods my soul
There are so many things
That I would love to say
Oh but if I only knew
the right words to pray

Heaven has entered at my door
As the tears reluctantly
Cease to fill my eyes
Oh how I wish that I could cry
As my soul longs for an answer
To a question why

Many feel they know me
They don't understand
Their intentions are right
But they are sincerely wrong
How can you come to where I've come
Except you have been to where I've been
Many feel this is a hard saying
So let me enlighten you
If there is any doubt
A man's heart is like a deep water
But it takes a man of understanding
To draw it out

AUTHOR: Linda M. Foster
Dated: 5/1/2000

HEAVEN AWAITS

There is a city made without hands
It is like a precious stone covered with jasper
and it's clear as crystal
This city that awaits me needs no sun nor moon
for it to shine in darkness
Because the glory of God shall be the light of it
The foundations of this city has been garnished with all manner
of different kinds of precious stones

That great city is pure gold like unto clear glass
Now therefore when all else has failed
Nothing seems to come together
When friends forsake me I will hold my head up high
for the world to see
But when in doubt
I will remember that city called Heaven

Written by: Linda M. Foster
Dated: 5/20/1999

HEAVEN'S TABLE

The night has gone away
A new day has just begun

Lately You have been far away from my mind
Making it hard for me to pray

It's hard to cope going through life's stages
Many are weak
And many sleep
By browsing through life's pages

My mind is not completely free
to please You as it should
Yet I feel Your awesome presence
That draws me nearer so I could

I would have asked You to let me sit at Your right hand
But You had spoken
It's not Mine to give
But My Father's plan

I would love to give You all
And heed to Your call
So make me pure
I know You can
I'm very sure
As You prepare me a feast
Pull me a chair towards the East
Although I am not stable
I know You are able
To make me ready
To sit at Heaven's table

AUTHOR: Linda M. Foster
Dated: 5/9/2000

HELPESS HURT

Thank you for the set up
It caused me not to give up

Thank you for the misguided plan

For it taught me not to trust any man

Thank you for the dry land
It helped me to stand

Thank for the pain
And the pouring down rain

Thank you for the ploy
It has restored its joy

Thank you for the flirt
Which was an insult
To a helpless hurt

AUTHOR: Linda M. Foster
Dated: 8/4/2001

HIGH INTELLECT

Intelligence is something that is learned in the mind
It is known by what you see and hear around you
It can be given by a speech or lecture
Or just by being taught by someone of intelligence

Intelligence is considered being smart
Being smart is not determined on how well you speak
Intellectual maturity is determined on how well you listen
when they speak

Intelligence is not boastful or proud
It is not arrogant haughty or even a proud look
Intelligence does not belittle people of lower degree
To make themselves feel or seem as though
they are better or exalted

Intelligence is just simple maturity
Maturity in the mind
In behavior
In speech
The use of wisdom and understanding in everyday life

Everyone has a different level of maturity
Some has outgrown others and some have not
Now I said all this to say this
Intelligence is not just how much you know or even considered
how much you have

It is determined by what you do with what you know or have
Use it wisely
When an intelligent one comes along and is boastful of oneself
The expense of other people who feels they are of a lower level
can become offended and

continued

May choose to disassociate or have no dealings with you
It's time to accept people where they are and
help build from there
For your life is not your own
Don't spend time just tooting your own horn
Be a giver of life to someone else who needs you and
can benefit
Because of your involvement with them

Author: Linda M. Foster
Dated: 7/1/2002

I worry

When you are away
I know I should pray
But instead I worry
Wishing you would come home in a hurry

AUTHOR: Linda M. Foster
Dated: 2/5/2000

I'LL RISE AGAIN

I'll rise above the ground
I'll rise above the waters across the seashore
And I'll come up on dry land for the floods will not drown me
And rivers will not drown me for I am in His perfect will

Verily I say unto you
The enemies which are the gain sayers
Go ahead laugh at me
Go ahead mock my destiny
Very soon you will see
For God has said when thou passeth through the waters
I'll be with thee

Also when thou go through the floods it will not over take thee
And if there be any fire that kindle upon thy soul shall not burn
For the light has come and the glory of God has risen
so you shall see
I shall rise again

AUTHOR: Linda M. Foster
Dated: 12/19/13

LONELY HEARTS CRY

Lonely hearts cry
Lonely hearts bleed for more
You really don't know what it's like
Until you have walked in someone else's shoes
Calling someone
No one answers
Waiting by the phone
It never rings
When it does
It is someone else
All hopes and dreams
were shattered

Lonely hearts cry
Lonely hearts bleed for more
It's not enough to say I love you
It's not enough just to say I care
When I deserve much more
I never asked you for money unless it was needed
I became a friend
Stayed by your side
When much is given much is required
When little is given little is required

Lonely hearts cry
Lonely hearts bleed for more
When loneliness takes over we as women sometimes run to men
And men sometimes run to women

Then there are some who just want to be a close friend
All in all misery loves company

continued

There's no loneliness like the one who's with someone
and still feel alone

I said all this to say this
You have to love yourself in order to feel comfortable
in being by yourself

AUTHOR: Linda M. Foster
DATED: 4/20/2001

MISSING YOU

Missing you is all I ever do
Oh how I long to hear your sweet gentle muscular voice
But I dare not even call you for you have given me no other choice

Missing you is so true
But with you that's nothing new
Although I know you come from afar
Wherever you are or where ever you may be
You are in remembrance of me
Your flight could be here and gone tomorrow
But in heart you are only a distance away

AUTHOR: Linda M. Foster
Dated: 6/15/13

OH LORD I PRAY

I bow before Thee
My eyes are closed
Hands lifted high
Oh Lord, I pray

Make my enemies my footstool
Let them not trample over me
And when they talk against me
Hide me
Cover me under the shadow of Thy wings
Show me the strength of salvation
Shower me with grace and truth
Oh lord, I pray

When my friends forsake me
They've all gone away
When they turn their backs on me
Lord, lift me up
And when my work is finished
It's all done
Bury me in paradise
When I reach that other side

Until then I'll keep on reaching
For I love You
With my soul
And all my strength
Therefore I love You
With my whole full life

AUTHOR: Linda M. Foster
Dated: 9/4/2000

OH MY! YOU HAVE A WAY WITH ME

I love the way You love me and proved Yourself to me
I also love the way You showed me
There's no one quite like You
I love the way You chosen me
My life long friend

There's no voice that I'd rather hear
You have a way with me
There's no other place that I'd rather be than with You
Your presence makes me whole

While I was feeling low
You came along and made me strong
You stood by me when no one else would

During my hardest times of life
While the tears fell from off the face of my cheeks
You embraced me with Your love
No one else could

In my time of mourning You came with healing in Your wings
My sorrow once again was turned into joy
Oh my! You have a way with me

AUTHOR: Linda M. Foster
Date: 4/20/1999

PRAYER OF TOGETHERNESS

Lord, make my husband and I one
Move back the dark clouds
that's covering us
Let spiritual rain come down from above
As we make preparations in our lives
So that you will be able to say
"Well done"

Lord, make our feet like hind
Prepare the way for us to be prosperous
Settle our hearts
And keep us in mind
For darkness was upon the face of the deep
There came a voice like many waters
It said, "Let there be light"
And the world now shineth

Lord, make us come together in unity
Let us not be divided any longer
As our love in You
grow stronger
Show us a new and better way
Teach him and me how to pray
With a firm desire
Daily by day

AMEN
Author: Linda M. Foster
Dated: 4/8/2000

REJOICE IN THE LORD

Stormy weather on a gloomy day
Flashing thunder lights in a dreary place
The sun comes out tomorrow
Each firming heat I would have to borrow
The cold snow flakes that fell to the ground
As I stand outside and look all around

When day comes
Night is not far behind
Storm clouds come and go
Just like your circumstances
You may be up today and down tomorrow
Or vice versa

Nevertheless nothing ever stays the same
But verily I say unto you
If thou should harken unto the voice of the Lord and do good
So shall thy be fed and thy house

Rejoice in hope
Do good so shall thy dwell in the land
And thou shall have plenty
More than enough
Be righteous
For I have made thee righteous through My grace and mercy

God came that He may save that which was lost
Hold on to your faith
For in due season you shall reap if you faint not
May the God of your calling sanctify you holy without blame
Until the coming of our Lord and savior Jesus Christ
the righteous
Who is Lord over all
Selah
Amen
AUTHOR: Linda M. Foster
DATE: 4/20/2000

REMEMBERING YOU

How can I forget
When each face that I see reminds me of being with you
Your face reluctantly appears in the rear of my mind
Wishing and hoping that one day I can be free from it

How can I forget your smile
Your touch and not to mention
the warmness of your embrace
Now that you are gone
Not by choice or any reason
But by an obligation you have left without a trace

How can I forget the summer or sunny day
The flowers that blossoms or trees that buds
And the rose in all it's splendid beauty
I haven't forgotten this is true
Just a thought today of all days
I just had to remember you

Author: Linda M. Foster
Dated 8/12/1999

Ruptured Plan

Although your plans have fallen through
It is nothing left for you to do
But try to undo the love that once grew
Between me and you

When sorrow has took it's place
And joy has hid it's face

When night is far apart
And the day is at hand
Then you will be able to stand

AUTHOR: Linda M. Foster
Dated: 2/20/2013

SACRED MARRIAGE

Being married is not an obligation
It's a choice
If you have not made that decision
Yet rejoice

Being married is a symbol of love
It's a gift from above
It's shared by male and female

Being married is not peaches and cream
As some suppose
Bet yet you are still a team

Being married
Sometimes the pressures of life
causes you to forget
what you really meant to each other
And it causes some to return to their mother
Don't be afraid to disagree
Talk it over while having tea

Being married
Many go through different stages of
uncertain security or surety
So lets find a cure to stay pure
Look back at some old photographs and laugh

Before you throw your arms up
And put your hand on your chin
Think back and remember when

Even though you have not continued to ride the carriage
It's still sacred marriage

AUTHOR: Linda M. Foster
Date: 10/6/2001

SAFETY

The greatest fears of male and female
is in the night
I too had this problem
But now I have seen the light
I will not be afraid any longer
For when I lay down and sleep
And then awakened
My God sustains me
So I am no longer bound
But I am free

The greatest fears of children
Are being in the dark by themselves
Every child needs to know
That God is their light and salvation
Of whom should they fear
God is the strength of their life
Of whom should they be afraid
We as people
Teach our children very little
About God's authority
We tend to teach them more about
Santa Claus and his elves

My greatest fear is not any of the above
But it is
Not being in the will of God
Now to whom it is
that does not know what this means
To them it will seem odd
My chances for terrible fear is slim
For the Angels of the Lord
Encampeth 'round about me
So you see

continued

When I lay down in peace and sleep
My Lord only makest me to dwell in safety

Author: Linda M. Foster
Dated: 7/3/2000

SEASONS CHANGE

If I had wings like a dove
I would fly away and be at rest
I could soar like the Eagles
I'll rise above the storm

If I had wings like a dove
I would outlast every storm
I would soar above the highest mountain
But only if I had wings

I dreamed a dream
I had wings like a dove
I flew away to be at rest
I soared like the Eagles above the storm

I dreamed a dream
I soared above the highest mountain
I dreamed a dream

Everything changes
We'll make it through somehow
Things are rearranging patiently endure
For nothing stays the same there will be better days I'm sure
We'll make it through somehow
For all seasons change

AUTHOR: Linda M. Foster
Dated: 6/2/1999

SINGING IN THE RAIN

I woke up early one morning
Fumbled out of my bed
I walked toward the restroom to wash my face
When I left the restroom
I dressed myself
Oh what a beautiful morning
Oh what a beautiful day

When I walked out my front door I looked up to Heaven
And what did I see
A band of Angels watching over me
Oh what a smile on my face you can't replace
Oh what a beautiful morning
Oh what a beautiful day

I walk down the street in the heat of the day
I looked around and what did I see
Flowers blooming everywhere
Everywhere grass is green
I'm singing
Oh what a beautiful morning
Oh what a beautiful day

AUTHOR: Linda M. Foster
Dated: 4/10/2013

SWEET WHISPERS OF LIES

One bright and sunny day while cleaning
I heard a whisper of words declared unto me
No one cares for you
Certain family members those who you were close to
are no longer
No one wants to be bothered
You are left all alone
Children are forgotten
You are not important nor special to anyone
But you still go on as if nothing ever happened

Shortly I began to look back
My circumstances seem overwhelming
I thought within myself maybe it's true
Nevertheless I knew it was whispers of the Deceiver
Who was a liar from the beginning
My life is not over
It has just begun

I have peace and uplifting joy
Not because I failed to listen because my ears were open
It's not that I didn't take heed 'cause it maybe true to
some point
But my God has not forsaken me
He has given me life, hope, and abundance of happiness
My sins are forgiven
I turn to Him

When no one would receive me
Words of utterance
When no one would hear I speak to Him
And if no one knows my grief or my heavy sorrow
His love will sustain me

Although family and friends may forsake me
My eyes will be lifted up
Great joy shall remain
As my arms stretch forth to Heaven my feet will not slip

For I may be many things
But there is one thing that I am not
And that is unloved
When in doubt the Lord shall truly bring me out
For my hope is built on nothing less than Jesus Christ and His righteousness
I dare not trust the sweetest frame
But wholly lean on Jesus name

Author: Linda M. Foster
DATED: 12/19/13

THE AMAZEMENT

I am amazed at what goes on in this world today
It makes me sometimes feel reluctant to stay
So I take one day after another day

I am amazed of people in the world today
My greatest need is to pray for guidance, strength,
And peace in the midst of turmoil and confusion
Last but not least
An unadulterated illusion

I am amazed of everyone
Not specific
But in general
Who pretend to be something they're not
I don't mean to be critical
But you have become my obstacle
Many of Christians are in the same situation
Take note
There is still hope
It's not that I have already overcome this test
And become my very best
When we recognize our heavenly vision
And secure our heavenly calling
Then we will began to make a decision
To end the amazement of people

AUTHOR: Linda M. Foster
DATE:2/6/1999

THE FAVOR OF GOD

Favor
Be my friend
Walk with me along the way
Where ever my feet shall tread

Favor
Look at me in my distress
When one says no
You say yes

Favor
It is not so much the big things that you do
But the small things
Which is clearly seen

Favor
You come from up above
So may God open the windows of Heaven
Pour you down on me that I may be successful in everything
that I do

Amen

Author: Linda M. Foster
Date: 12/19/13

"THE GOD OF ALL COMFORT"

May the Lord above preserve and keep you
May His love and kindness surround your heart
then cover you like a blanket
May the Holy Spirit comfort and guide you
May you lay your head upon His breast and rest
as if it were your very own tender pillow

May the overcomer in you arise and stand strong
against all odds
May the Lord shine brightly upon your countenance
in this dark hour of despair and disappointment

May He gently lavish His love upon you continually
May His peace fill your heart and rest upon you like a dove
May the Angels in Heaven gather together
All around bringing you into joy and laughter
once again in thee appointed time

May the joy of the Lord be your strength
while moving sorrow, discomfort, and uneasiness from
your heart
May the Word of God that abides in you endure
And may His sweet presence be with you everywhere you go
It is documented in the Holy scriptures
Jesus said unto Martha
"I am the resurrection and the life
He that believeth in Me,
Though he were dead
Yet shall he live."
Therefore to be absent from the body
Is to be present with the Lord

I declare there is a city made without hands
having the glory of God
Her light

It's like a precious stone and also jasper
It's clear as crystal
The street of this city is pure gold
like transparent glass
For the Lord almighty and the Lamb are it's temple
This city needs no sun or moon to shine
For the glory of God illuminates it
Therefore the nations of those who are saved
shall walk in it

AUTHOR: Linda M. Foster
Written: 8/14/2014

THE ROAR OF THUNDER

When the thunder roars
Many say that God is talking
It gives a loud boom sound
And frightens mostly everyone
Especially those who are walking

When the thunder is increased
With lightening flashes
It causes many people to wonder
I myself eagerly await
Hoping and praying
That it would cease or become asunder

Thunder and lightening
Causes many to fear and tremble
They become afraid for their lives
And the things around them
That they own
Although I know God's love surrounds me
I put Him in remembrance of thee
During the roar of thunder

AUTHOR: Linda M. Foster
Dated: 7/5/2000

TRADING PLACES

There are some people who believe that love never dies
And there are some who believe that once your heart has been
trampled on
There is nothing in the world you can ever do to bring it back

Can love turn to hate?
That's the question we as people sometimes ask
Love is strong and it is powerful
It can stand through the toughest time
Love can go through the fire and move through the floods
Now unto whom is able to understand
Watch as well as pray

Now there was a certain man who abused that love someone
had for him
He did not appreciate the goodness in her
Now the love she had turned cold
You may say that wasn't love
Well when love has entered your heart it stays forever
But because your mind starts to wonder or accuse and it tells
you enough is enough
The members in your body gets the message
Then it starts to react accordingly to what your mind is saying
Then it enters into your heart
Your mind is the window to your heart
But your heart is the door to your soul
Many don't understand this saying, but to whom it is given does
Love is kind and is not puffed up
Love rules oneself and not another

Love to my knowledge can turn to hate
You may remember the good times and ignore the bad
But you just can't live off of good memories
So the question is not do you love him or her
The question is who do you love more

So the conclusion of the whole matter is
The proof is in the pudding
When love turns
That's just a simple phrase
So if your love ever turned to hate
You just simply traded places

Written by: Linda M. Foster
Date: 2/18/1999

TRUE LOVE

On the cool of the day
While lying in my bed
As my child cries I'm tired and longing to rest
He leaves the room not quite at his best
My eyes closed and sleep fell upon me
When my eye lids opened
Thoughts fluttered my mind suddenly like a rushing
mighty wind
I thought within myself
What is love?
My mind begin to wonder and the answers flood my soul
Love takes the place of another
It is not jealous or puffed up
It is kind and confident of oneself
Love stands through the toughest of times
It suffers long and it endures
Love forgives the unforgettable
It rest assures
It gains respect of the one who receives it
Love is not based on what you can feel alone
Even though some believe it's love
because it feels good or seems right
But yet hold on to it with all your might
Love is stable in it's security
Although love is said by many
It's only given by few
Many do not know what it means to be in love
Love is a verb
It's action
Love stands when passion has ceased
When your heart no longer goes pity pat
When beauty is gone and goose bumps are no longer found
So no matter where or who you are
Before you say I love you
True love never dies

Written By: Linda M. Foster
Dated: 2/20/13

WHO ART THOU

Who art thou, O Lord
That Thy art mindful of me
Who art thou, O Lord
That thou shouldest send me
Who art thou, O Lord
That mighty men marvel at Your greatness
And host of Angels
Sing in Your presence
As kings rush to kneel at Your feet
Who art thou, O Lord
The world wonders
At Thy hand
The blind receive their sight
In Thy own name
The lame began to walk
A deaf ear can hear
And also the dumb speak
While the poor has the gospel preached
unto them
Who art thou, O Lord
That the world is amazed

When there were no fishes in the sea
Nor moon or stars to appear in the sky
Neither any birds to fly in the air
You were there
Who art thou, O Lord
I sometimes wonder
Even the children's children
Hope thou in You
Many believe and yet have not seen
As I believe
They tell me of a home so far away
Where the Eagles
Dare not try to fly
Who art thou, O Lord

continued

That thou art mindful of these
And He answers
Verily I say unto you
Therefore I am the Lord thy God
That heareth thee
Walk by faith and not by sight
He who walks alone
Will receive strength
And endure power
From on high
So endure hardness as a good soldier
Look not unto the right or to the left
Focus your eyes on the One who rules above
Look unto the hill from whence cometh
your help
Your help cometh from the Lord
Which made Heaven and Earth
He who heeds to wise words
Will increase in learning
A wise man will hear
But a foolish one
Will run from it
Because pride has entered into the heart
But whosoever
Hearken unto the voice of the Lord
Thou shall be safe from all fear of evil

AUTHOR: Linda M. Foster
DATED: 9/1/2001

WHY ME

"Why?"
Is a question we have all asked
Once or more in our life time
If we knew the reason for the situation
We may feel that we can cope with it better
But the Lord only knows
With Him not anything goes
So don't feel abandoned or dismayed
'cause most things are best left unlearned
Please don't feel neglected or betrayed
For God is still concerned

AUTHOR: Linda M. Foster
Dated: 5/2/2000

WORDS OF HOPE

Arise from your dead ashes
Turn not to the right nor to the left
Walk through the desert
'till thou has found thy water
flowing from the rocks
toward an empty cave

Fill thy cup with water
Anoint thy head with oil
Enter into thy closet
Take thy shoes from off thy feet

Reach where thou has not reached
Sow where thou has not sown
Arise from thy youth as the Eagles stand ground
Offer unto Thee sacrifices of praise
Recognize thy calling
Move towards thy destination
When thou has laid upon thy bed
be still and know that I am God
Arise I say
Verily I say unto you
Arise

Written by: Linda M. Foster
Date: 2/18/1999

LAND OF FREEDOM

May God bless America through change
From the White House to the State Capital
Federal Officials
City Officials
To all the people and surrounding cities
May we stand strong and united in freedom
May He deliver this great nation from oppression, depression,
and poverty
May we all come under the grace of His saving knowledge
May this country continue to uphold the law with kindness,
mercy, and justice for all people
May God bless Israel and send peace to Jerusalem
May we serve the only true God
The Creator of Heaven and Earth
Turn from false Gods of hatred
Agree to disagree
Live in love and peace toward one another
Turn from just religion alone
Have fellowship with Him
The Lord Emanuel
meaning God with us
Selah! Amen.

Written By: Linda M. Foster
Date: 2/11/2013

CITATION QUOTES

Page 13: "Therefore I am somebody more than a conquer through Him that loved me." New International Version Romans 8:37

Page 14: "From dust you came and from dust ye shall return." American King James Version Genesis 3:19

Page 18: "Though their sin be as scarlet they shall be white as snow, though they be red like crimson they shall be as wool." New International Version Isaiah 1:18

Page 18: "Blow the trumpet in Zion, sound the alarm on My Holy mountain." English Standard Version Joel 2:1

Page 19: "I am the vine you are the branches." New International Version John Chapter 15:5

Page 19: "For I am the bread of life which came down from heaven." New International Version John Chapter 6:51

Page 19 "Be rooted and grounded." New King James Version Ephesians Chapter 3:17

Page 19 "Be like the tree planted by the rivers of water that bring forth fruit in its season." King James Bible Psalm Chapter 1:3

Page 19 "Your leaf shall not whither and whatever you do shall prosper." King James Bible Psalm Chapter 1:3

Page 19 "I will go before you and make the crooked places straight." King James Version Isaiah 45:2

Page 21 "Why do you search for the living among the dead, He is not here, He has risen just as Christ said He would." New International Version Luke Chapter 24:5-6

Page 23: "Pride goes before destruction and a haughty spirit before a fall." New International Version Proverbs Chapter 16:18

Page 25: "A Good name is rather to be chosen than great riches." KJV Proverbs Chapter 22:1

Page 27: "train you up in the way that you should go for when you are old he or she will not depart from the truth." New King James Version Proverbs Chapter 22:6

Page 28 "He has given Hos angels charge concerning thee." King James Bible Psalm 91:11

Page 32: "Give unto Caesar the things that are Caesar's and give God the things that are His."   NET Bible Mark Chapter 12:17

Page 35: "A man's heart is like deep water but it takes a man of understanding to draw it out."

Page 42: "For the light has come and the glory of God has risen." King James Version Isaiah Chapter 60:1

Page 46 "Cover me under the shadow of Thy wings."

Page 48 "Let there be light." King James Version Genesis Chapter 1:3

Page 49 "You shall reap if you faint not." King James Version Chapter 6:9

Page 49 "God came that He may save that which was lost." American King James Version Luke 19:10

Page 53 "God is their light and salvation of whom should they fear." New International Version Psalm Chapter 27:1

Page 53: "For the angels of the Lord encampeth 'round about me." New King James Version Psalm Chapter 34:7

Page 53 "God is the strength of their life of whom should they be afraid." King James Bible Psalm Chapter 27:1

Page 58 "I dare not trust the sweetest frame but wholly lean on Jesus name" Cornerstone Edward Mote song Published 1937

Page 61 "I am the resurrection and the life, He that believeth in Me though he were dead yet shall he live." King James Bible John Chapter 11:25

Page 68 "Walk by faith and not by sight." New King James Version 2 Corinthians Chapter 5:7

Page "Look unto the hill from whence cometh your help." King James Version Psalm Chapter 121:1

CPSIA information can be obtained
at www.ICGtesting.com
Printed in the USA
LVOW04s0518040216

473600LV00010B/28/P